Glorious Flowers

COLORING BOOK

SIRIUS

SIRIUS

This edition published in 2022 by Sirius Publishing, a division of
Arcturus Publishing Limited,
26/27 Bickels Yard, 151–153 Bermondsey Street,
London SE1 3HA

ISBN: 978-1-3988-2130-9
CH005274NT
Supplier 29, Date 0422, PI 00001861

Printed in China

Introduction

Flowers have always made fascinating subjects for artists and they are a wonderful challenge to reproduce. Following on from the first title, *Coloring Flowers*, this book contains a selection of more than 40 beautiful flower paintings by renowned botanical artists for you to color.

The simple line drawings are reproduced directly from the artists' sketches and are waiting for you to add all the necessary color and detail. Remember, there's no better way to learn than by copying the masters.

Watercolor paint or colored pencils are the best mediums to use for these illustrations – you may find the latter easier. Be sure to blend your colors and follow the natural direction of the subject's textures, working along the lines of the leaves and petals to faithfully re-create these natural wonders.

All of the artwork in this book has been drawn from either the *L'Illustration horticole*, a 19th-century Belgian journal founded by Jean Jules Linden in 1854 and illustrated by some of the finest botanical artists and lithographers of the day, including A. Goossens, P. De Pannemaeker and J. Goffart; or from *Choix des plus belles Fleurs* (*Choice of the Most Beautiful Flowers*), published in 1827 and illustrated by Pierre-Joseph Redouté. A one-time court artist to Marie Antoinette, Redouté illustrated more than 1800 plant species and remains one of the most famous artists in the genre of botanical painting to this day.

Where available, the Latin names that were provided by the original 19th-century artists have been included underneath each color illustration. The common names are also provided below each line drawing. With such an array of exquisite illustrations to study, you cannot fail to be inspired in your own endeavors.

Key: *List of plates*

1 *Aster chinensis*
(China aster)

2 *Lilas* (Lilac)

3 *Gentiana acaulis*
(Gentian)

4 *Lilium bulbiferum*
(Tiger lily)

5 *Rosa indica*
(Indian rose)

6 *Lonicera*
(Honeysuckle)

7 *Gazania splendens*
(Treasure flower)

8 *Centaurea cyanus*
(Cornflower)

9 *Digitalis purpurea*
(Common foxglove)

10 *Primula auricula*
(Bouquet of primulas)

11 *Hortensia*
(Hydrangea)

12 Hellebore and
carnations

13 *Cheiranthus flavus*
(Wallflower)

14 *Anemone stellata*
(Broad-leaved anemone)

15 Bouquet of rose,
anenome and clematis

16 *Tagetes* (Marigold)

17 *Dianthus albo-nigricans*
(Sweet William)

18 *Crocus sativus*
(Saffron crocus)

19 Varieties of *Nigella
hispanica (Love-in-a-mist)*

20 *Rosa gallica
aurelianensis*
(La Duchesse d'Orléans)

21 *Coreopsis elegans*
(Tickseed)

22 *Aquilegia spectabilis*
(Columbine)

23 *Primula sinensis*
(Chinese primrose)

24 *Tropaeolum majus*
(Nasturtium)

25 *Azalea indica gigantiflora* (Azalea)

26 *Primavera grandiflora* (Primrose)

27 Bouquet of pansies

28 *Lathyrus latifolius* (Everlasting pea)

29 *Ixia viridiflora* (Turquoise ixia)

30 Geranium variety

31 *Petunia inimitabilis* (Petunia)

32 *Geum coccineum* (Dwarf orange avens)

33 *Plumbage caerulea* (Plumbago)

34 Double dahlia

35 *Gladiolus cuspidatus* (Corn flag)

36 *Fuchsia solferino* (Fuchsia)

37 *Cactus grandiflorus* (Night-blooming cereus)

38 *Rosa pomponia* (Pompon rose)

39 *Phlox reptans* (Phlox)

40 *Punica granatum* var. *legrelliae* (Flowering pomegranate)

41 *Platylobium* (Flat-pea)

42 *Lechenaultia biloba* (Blue lechenaultia)

43 *Lavatera phoenicea* (Tree mallow)

44 Bouquet of roses

Aster chinensis

China aster

Lilas

Lilac

Gentiana acaulis

Gentian

Lilium bulbiferum

Tiger lily

Rosa indica

Indian rose

Lonicera

Honeysuckle

Gazania splendens

Treasure flower

Centaurea cyanus

Cornflower

Digitalis purpurea

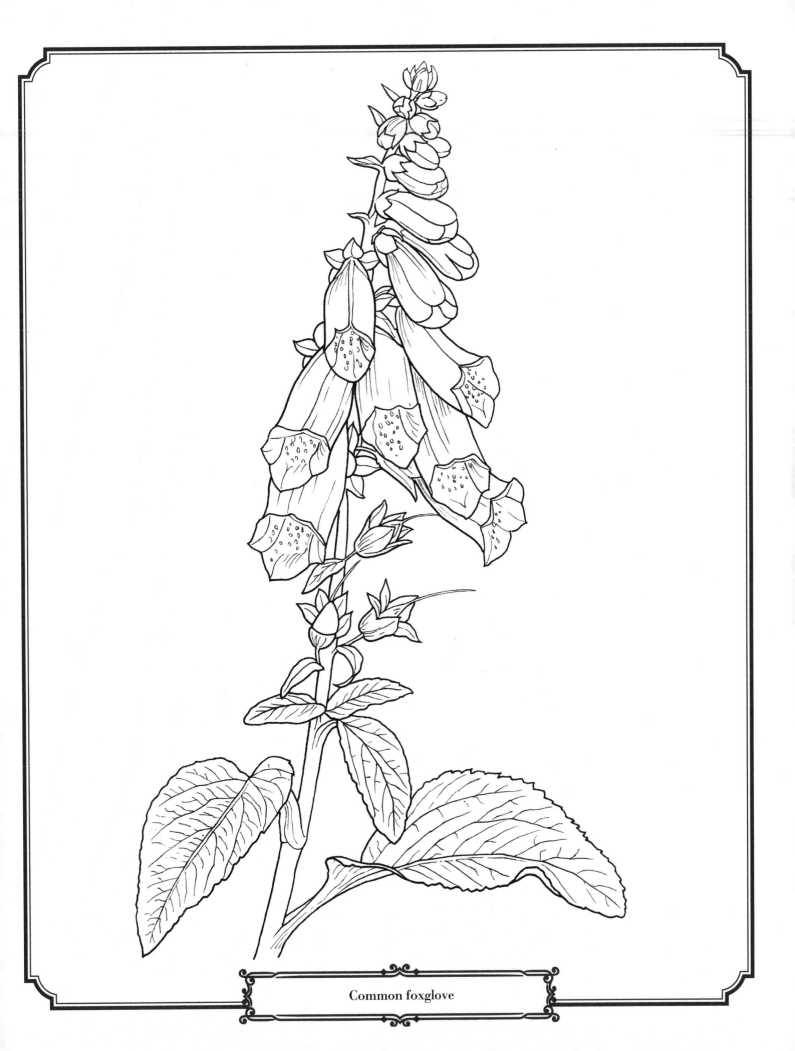

Common foxglove

Primula auricula

Bouquet of primulas

Hortensia

Hydrangea

Hellebore and carnations

Hellebore and carnations

Cheiranthus flavus

Wallflower

Anemone stellata

Broad-leaved anemone

Bouquet of rose, anenome and clematis

Bouquet of rose, anenome and clematis

Tagetes

Marigold

Dianthus albo-nigricans

Sweet William

Crocus sativus

Saffron crocus

Varieties of Nigella hispanica

Love-in-a-mist

Rosa gallica aurelianensis

La Duchesse d'Orléans

Coreopsis elegans

Tickseed

Aquilegia spectabilis

Columbine

Primula sinensis

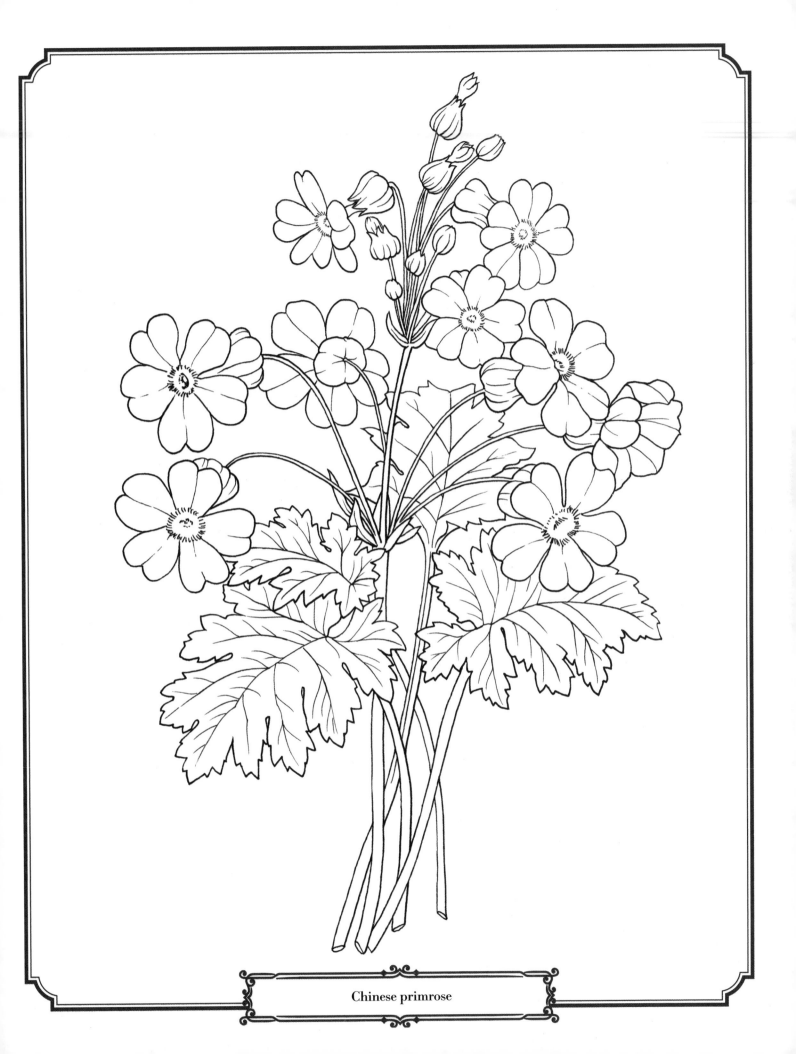

Chinese primrose

Tropaeolum majus

Nasturtium

Azalea indica gigantiflora

Azalea

Primavera grandiflora

Primrose

Bouquet of pansies

Bouquet of pansies

Lathyrus latifolius

Everlasting pea

Ixia viridiflora

Turquoise ixia

Geranium variety

Geranium variety

Petunia inimitabilis

Petunia

Geum coccineum

Dwarf orange avens

Plumbage caerulea

Plumbago

Double dahlia

Double dahlia

Gladiolus cuspidatus

Corn flag

Fuchsia solferino

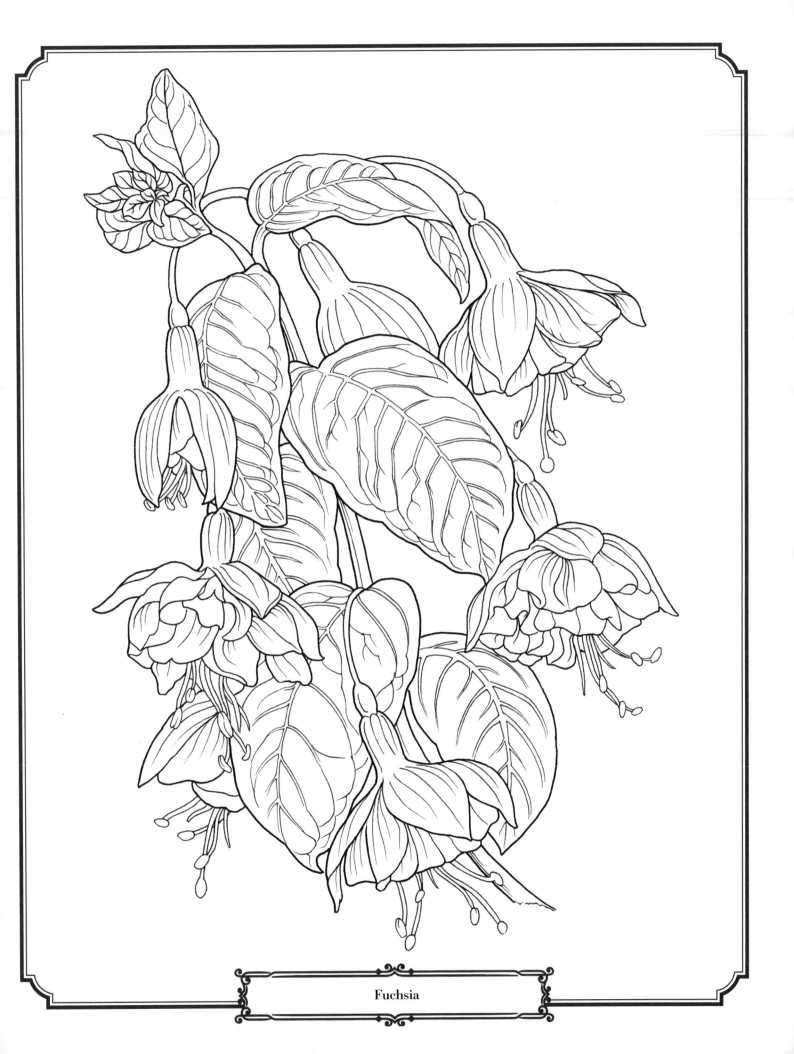

Fuchsia

Cactus grandiflorus

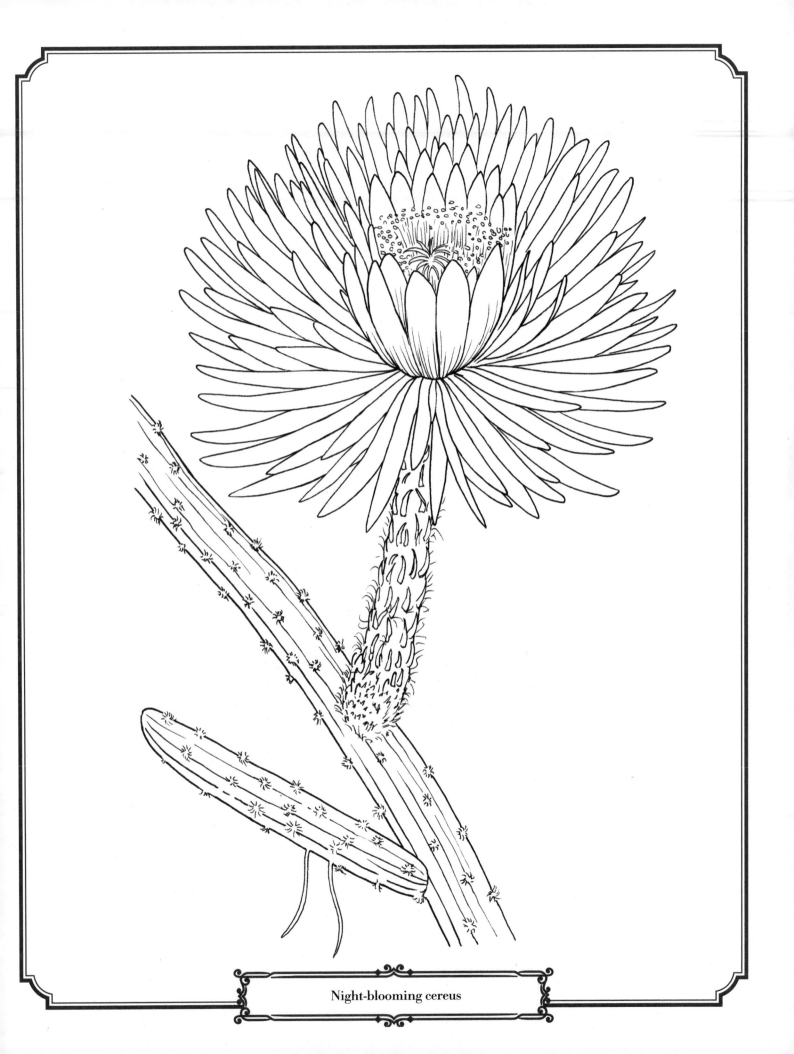

Night-blooming cereus

Rosa pomponia

Pompon rose

Phlox reptans

Phlox

Punica grantum var. *legrelliae*

Flowering pomegranate

Platylobium

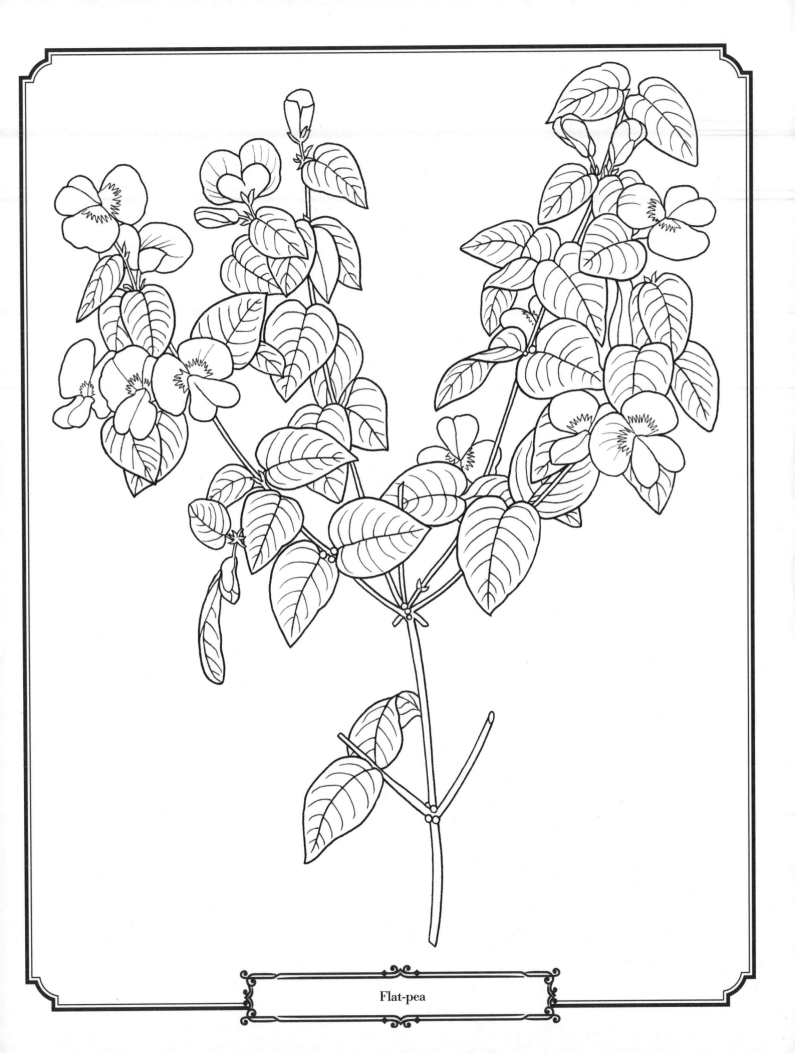

Flat-pea

Lechenaultia biloba

Blue lechenaultia

Lavatera phoenicea

Tree mallow

Bouquet of roses

Bouquet of roses